THE NEXT ONE
THOUSAND YEARS

THE NEXT ONE
THOUSAND YEARS

THE SELECTED POEMS OF
CID CORMAN

EDITED BY
CE ROSENOW &
BOB ARNOLD

LONGHOUSE

First Edition

Copyright © 2008 by Bob Arnold, Literary Executor for the
Estate of Cid Corman

Preface copyright © 2008 by Ce Rosenow
Afterword copyright © 2008 by Bob Arnold

Cover photograph: Haguro-san steps
copyright © 2008 by Dobree Adams
Frontispiece sketch copyright © 2008 by Bob Arnold
Back cover photograph of Cid Corman, a gift to
Bob Arnold (photographer unknown).
Book design by *two-hands* & Jonathan Greene

Published & distributed by

Longhouse, Publishers & Booksellers
1604 River Road
Guilford, Vermont 05301

Email : poetry@sover.net
www.LonghousePoetry.com

Library of Congress Cataloging-in-Publication Data

Corman, Cid.
    The next one thousand years : the selected poems of Cid
Corman / edited by Bob Arnold & Ce Rosenow. – 1st ed.
        p. cm.
    ISBN-13: 978-1-929048-08-3 (alk. paper)
    ISBN-10: 1-929048-08-4 (alk. paper)
    I. Arnold, Bob, 1952- II. Rosenow, Ce III. Title.
PS3553.O65N49 2008
811'.54--dc22

                                                    2007052674

for Shizumi

CONTENTS

PUBLISHER'S NOTE

We would like to extend our thanks to all the editors and publishers of the many books where we lustfully selected poems of Cid's. This range of books begins with Cid Corman's own *Origin Press*, James L. Weil's *The Elizabeth Press*, Bob Arnold's *Longhouse*, John Martone's *tel-let*, Jonathan Greene's *Gnomon Press* and many many more. Some publications are as small as a folded napkin. Cid was one for overlapping many of his books with some of the same poems, or even different versions of the same poems, book to book. To calculate this poet's navigation is fruitless – he gave and he received and the poems were almost always the greatest gift.

We also bow in thanks to the following people for their care and support: Susan Arnold, Ed Baker, Puiyin Chiu, Shizumi Corman, Darrin Daniel, David Giannini, Jonathan Greene, Gerald Hausman, Stefan Hyner, Louise Landes Levi, Kalah McCaffrey, John Martone, Charlie Mehrhoff, Julie Moffenbier, Erik Muller, J.P. Seaton, F.J. Seligson, David Shapiro, Helen Southworth, Angie Thompson, Michael Dylan Welch, and Laura Winter.

And, finally, our thanks to the Oregon Humanities Center and the Robert D. Clark Honors College for helping to make this publication possible.

Those interested in a further reading of Cid Corman's

versions of Japanese haiku might seek out the expanded
One Man's Moon published by Gnomon Press. For many
more Cid Corman books:

http://www.longhousepoetry.com/corman.html

PREFACE

Cid Corman wrote poetry on a daily basis for more than half a century. Through poetry, he acknowledged the unique, individual moments that make up our lives, and writing and rewriting these moments gave him insights into human nature and the human experience. His poems allowed him to communicate those insights to others. Corman's daily writing practice yielded a large body of work that circulated in broadsides, chapbooks, and volumes from both small presses and large publishers. Many of his numerous correspondents also received poems in Corman's letters, in some cases typed on the envelopes. When Corman died in 2004, his published works numbered in the hundreds.

Born in Boston in 1924, Corman completed a BA at Tufts University in 1945, pursued further studies at the University of Michigan and the University of North Carolina, Chapel Hill, and received a Fulbright Fellowship to study at the Sorbonne in 1954-55. His serious study of poetry provided him with extensive knowledge of poetic traditions and formal tools from which to draw when developing his own poetics. As Robert Creeley once stated, "His authority has been earned absolutely." Corman's knowledge of poetic traditions contributed to his translations, as well. He translated from many languages including Chinese, French, German, and Japanese, and interspersed his translations with original poetry in most of his books. These translations reflect Corman's belief that if one word of a poem is changed, the result is an entirely new poem. This belief led him to coin a new term for his translation process – transvising – and it also explains why, when publishing his transvisions, he often omitted the name of the original author.

During and after his education, Corman traveled widely and lived for a time in France and in Italy before moving to Kyoto, Japan where he married Shizumi Konishi. The Cormans made occasional visits to the U.S. and relocated to Boston from 1970-1982 before returning to Kyoto as their primary residence. Travel contributed to Corman's belief in the universality of human experience, an important theme in his poetry. The foundation of this universality is the fact that, while everyone is born and everyone will die, these two experiences actually co-exist within each single moment of one's life. Corman created the term, "livingdying," to express this co-existence, and he used his focus on the individual moments he personally experienced in countries around the world as a means of expressing "livingdying" in his work.

Corman's commitment to writing poetry was matched only by his dedication to circulating the work of other poets first through his radio program, "This is Poetry," on WMEX in Boston (1949-1951) and then through his publication, Origin, and his publishing company, Origin Press. He was preparing a sixth series of Origin when he passed away in Kyoto in 2004. Bob Arnold took on the editorship of the series, publishing four sweeping volumes as well as a coda in 2007, which amounted to exactly the same scope and page range as one of Cid's twenty-issue series of the past. As an editor and publisher, Cid supported the work of poets such as William Bronk, Robert Creeley, Denise Levertov, and Louis Zukofsky, who shared his interest in the particular and in revealing the significant within the common.

The size and range of Corman's body of work makes the creation of a new selected edition of his poetry a formidable task; it is, nonetheless, a timely and important one because the majority of Corman's books are out-of-print. In selecting the poems for this edition, we included those featuring the characteristics for which Corman is best known such as long, narrow verses built of short and often enjambed lines, word play, and direct address to the reader; however, we also wanted to acknowledge the breadth of Corman's poetic style by including everything from shorter, haiku-like poems to substantially longer poems and poems with traditionally-structured stanzas. Additionally, we incorporated a range of his translations and present them side-by-side with his own poems. Finally, we wanted to offer something new to longtime readers of Corman's work and so included poems from rare, privately circulated editions and three unpublished manuscripts: *OF* Vols. 4 and 5 and an untitled manuscript.

In an effort to be as thorough as possible in our selection process, Bob Arnold and I considered the approaches taken by the editors of the two earlier and important selected editions of Corman's poetry: *Words for Each*

Other (1967) and *Aegis* (1983). We also contacted numerous poets who were closely connected to Corman's work to ask for their recommendations. Finally, because we had access to so many of Corman's published books, we simply immersed ourselves in his poetry, trading discoveries and suggestions. Ultimately, we hope that this edition will offer readers a fulfilling experience with Corman's poetry by allowing them to spend time with a wide selection of Cid Corman's own words.

—Ce Rosenow

THE NEXT ONE
THOUSAND YEARS

Poetry
is all there

is – so come
and get it.

Wordpeople – one more
signified among
the signifiers.

THE DEATH OF

Before the word – more
than any voice – the
nothing breaking forth –

again and again –
he floated on with –
more penetrating

into more was he
penetrated by –
the more elusive

the word still the word –
he could not – might not
hold fast to it – in –

comprehensible –
unutterable –
the word beyond speech.

HERMANN BROCH

ADORNO

Poetry
after Auschwitz?

Poetry
after Eden?

Life remains
remembering.

NY 1934

You might ve thought she
was from Brooklyn when
asked by one of the

journalists: "Why dont
you write the way you
talk?" she replied as

only a Gertrude
Stein would: "Why dont you
read the way I write?"

TEEN
WEANING

I was very young –
9th grade – when the drunk
on the El got off

where I did and said
to any one young
enough to listen –

*Don't ever fall in
love.* But I was born –
alas – already.

the gift

first night in a
strange town to
be going home

passing a
strange girl saying
goodnight to me

how night is
when she says so
suddenly good

Spring dusk

Full moon
Girls seem

to be

circling
around

a shrine

Bury me
in your heart –
let me be

word of no
word – let the
breath occur.

Men women
and the shadows too
dancing.

'PSALM IV'

O love –
no
prayer –

be what
you –
pray – are.

PASSO

Virgin in crinoline,
virgin of la Soledad,
wideopen like an immense
tulip.

In your bark of light
go
through the high tide
of the city,
amidst saetas confused
and stars of crystal.
Virgin in crinoline,
you go
through the street's river
down to the sea!

THAN

milk whiter
water sweeter
harp more sounding
horse haughtier
roses more beautiful
himation softer
gold more worth

You are so nicely
into the weave you wear and
beyond undoing –
ah to be woven with
you – to have become that close.

'THE EXERCISE'

Shizumi

from the height
of the nuns'

temple steps

running down
as the sun

sets to me.

GOING
OUT

You take my beret
from the table – we
are ready now to

go out – on tiptoe
set it on my head
smiling together.

Do you know
what it means
to know what

it means to
be with you,
dear? I do.

SHIZUMI

We can sense beyond
any difference
that we who have found
love will also find
words for each other.

L'AMANTE / THE LOVER

for M.C.C.

So much had passion seized me for this delectable lover,
I not exempt from effusion and vibrant lubricity, I was,
was not to have died quietly or toned down, acknowledged
merely by my lover's eyelids. Nights of a wild novelty
had rediscovered the ardent communicating saliva, and
perfumed her feverish belonging. Thousands of adulterated
precautions invited me to the most voluptuous flesh ever.
In our hands a desire from beyond destiny, what fear at
our lips tomorrow?

RENÉ CHAR

LONG DISTANCE

My brother awoke
one night, I'm told,
and said to a sound

moved, 'Is that you, Cid?'
I'm here, of course –
whatever that means.

The father
cuts the wood –
the child's truck
stands waiting.

The snow is melting
the village is brimming with
all at once children.

Father and son
at night on a slope
resting against hay

gazed upon by stars
finding the needle
breath of their breath.

Children in groups with
their hands in one another's
in the fields of spring
in gathering tender greens
happy as happy can be.

My daughter grows
more beautiful
every day

and make me feel
more beautiful
in her growing.

The fact of my
having no child
doesnt change this.

Day is done, and we too have been brought into play
with the clothes and the shoes and the faces we had.
The hares have gone to their burrows and the cocks crow,
the face of my mother returns to the fireplace.

Sunset coming down the hill
The moon accompanying
Looking back vanishing trail
Horizon a deepened blue
You lead me by the hand home
Children let the rush blinds fall
On the bamboo and the path
Vines no longer grabbing us
Great to be able to rest
Share the pleasure of real wine
Singing like wind in the pine
Till voices fail and stars pale
And I am drunk you merry
And nothing of us remains

AFTER
AFTER

Nothing to be said
nothing being said

Sipping at mountains
watching water fall

Sweeping the garden
a rock striking bamboo and
everything clicks.

Lost in a dreamworld
and once again the dream ends
grass for a pillow
awakening all alone
having to think of it too.

People like Rembrandt
make my day. He looks
at me with a faint

smile – without pity
and without contempt.
He knows what I know

and knows I know. Do
you know what it means
just to have a friend?

OLD
FOLKS

Face wrinkles double-chin slack jowls
dark spotted skin, back bent, bald-headed,
grizzled white beard, hands trembling,
legs tottering, teeth gone, hearing hard,
eyesight dim. Needed are caps berets hoods,
jackets, mufflers, coats, glasses, canes,
hotwater bottles, hot blankets, pisspot,
back-scratcher. Fussbudget, always fearful of
dying, being alone, avoided, wary of all,
wanting all. The same words endlessly,
quick to anger and quick to fret, nothing
but complaint and lament, nothing is what
it was, bugging everyone and knowing all,
the same old story, the wonderful grandkids,
proud of longlife, wearing the youngers out.

SENGAI

'WCW
&
Mary O'

We stood up to go –

Bill too – wavering
and fragile – once straight

and tall – but when I

kissed him it was – as
it always had been –

is – a young man's kiss.

Suddenly
a bird call
makes it seem

(I dont know
why) like a
holiday –

like getting
a letter
from Lorine.

CINCINNATI

The hatred the
bum greeted me
with – in passing –

each a stranger
to the other –
brings my eyes tears –

for one enough
like me to be
me made him feel

like that. Now years
later I see
I met a friend.

Tsuji-sensei – that first time
at his house together – up
all night talking in gestures –

unrolled his Tessai scrolls
to show me what he meant – he
meaning himself and Tessai –

and I saw imagined streams –
pure white paper – streaming twice
down the steepest summits in

remotest China – mingling
in a common emptiness
just where we sat on the floor.

I am sitting here
and writing what should be
a poem for you.

I cannot explain –
there are tears in my eyes –
as if I were moved

by a profound loss,
not that of loneliness,
but of a silence

whose voice reminds me
of yours. You are sitting
writing a poem.

What can I do – friends?
I am the nothing
I am. Not a Jew –
not a Christian or
Jain or Muslim or
Hindu Buddhist – you
name it. Neither of
East or West – nor land
nor sea. Nor of earth
fire water or air –
neither bare ground nor
high throne – without a
nation anywhere –
this world or what next –
heaven or hell – no
place and no trace. No
body and no soul.
All my life yours – love.

Without you
no shadow
and the night

night. To see
heaven one
wants a star.

Not much to say now.
Was there ever?
Gently. The heart has

never been as much
given to words
as to sighs. Alas –

the softest cry calls
from night to night
softer and so soft.

KOMACHI

Was it only a

sleep would ever have brought him

to me? Had I known

it was all a dream I'd not

have bothered to awaken.

What can a
young man say
to an

old man
dying but
I die too

though nothing
in fact
is said.

The trouble

with the end –
as we all

know too well –

is that it's
only the

beginning,

Wherever you go
is the one shrine the
one altar the one

offering. Your death
in return for a
taste of this one life.

RUMI

THE GRACE

Thank you for
whatever
it is – just
as it is

Ah – if we
could only
leave it at
that – at this.

Life is re-

membering

and dont you

forget it.

YUP

Typical of me

telling you the obvious –

what you dont want to know.

What are we
waiting for?
The silence
is ready.

THE

mosquito
at the ear
saying so
so and so.

JOB

Patience is
rewarded:
nothing comes.

Empty air

exhaustless –
the more the

less the less

the more – speak
silence – keep

emptiness.

LAO TSE

53

BLABBERMOUTH

Everyone's
got to know.
Life is the

secret we
all want to
but can't keep.

NEW
PROVERBS

None can never have
enough of one.

A man in the woods
a man in the wild.

Pig in the pantry
pork in the pie.

Every snowflake
surrenders.

Any moment
yields as much.

Dont ask more of yourself
than the mirror does.

Perfection breeds contempt.

All truth is in vain.

The bee goes for the honey
despite the rose.

We are the nuts of the money tree.

A life taken
is a life lost.

Who amounts to none
amounts to all.

Each breath is
the breath of a sun.

Just resting –
letting the
breezes make

a thing of
a body –

The bridge flowing
water staying
wading clouds

Bring me the sunflower to transplant
in my soil parched by the salt air,
and let it show all day to the mirroring blues
of the sky the yearning of its yellowy face.

Things obscure tend to clarity,
exhaust their bodies in a flowing
of colors: these in musics. To fade
is thus the venture of ventures.

Bring me (dear) the plant that leads to
where blond transparencies arise
and life evaporates as essence;
bring me the sunflower crazed by light.

EUGENIO MONTALE

Though you say you'll come
more often than not you don't –
since you say and don't
I won't expect you to come
unless you say that you won't.

'Just
For
Now'

Remembering how

much I've forgotten reminds

me of this moment.

It all comes

back to this.

In fact – it

never left.

CHATEAU DE MUZOT

I may count myself
amongst the old but
in the nature of

these poems they must
be grasped by the breath by
those who share it. Two

experiences
produced them – one – to
hold life open to

death – and the other –
spiritual need
to situate love's

transfigurations
in this opening.
Whatever meaning

there is will be in
the stance of standing
strong in the foreground.

RAINER MARIA RILKE

If these words be ours
and the words nothing –
as they are – then we

are nothing too. Yes –
yes – let it be so.
But let the words know.

Poetry becomes

that conversation we could

not otherwise have.

IN
SUMMARY

The point of poetry is poetry –
but try telling that to the translators.
They bristle and cringe – whinge and cry snob – yet

life is meaningless without life itself
renewed and renewing. If you must speak –
let the breath lift from the breath meaning's word.

Nothing
lasts forever

That's the trouble
with it.

WHY THE DAY FLIES

The poet depends, during his life time, upon some
tree, or sea, or slope, or cloud of a certain tinge,
for a moment, if circumstance so wills. He isnt welded
to the bewilderment of others. His love, his grasp, his
bliss have their equivalent in all the places he has
never gone and never will go, amongst strangers he
will never know. When a voice is lifted unto him,
when he is urged to accent considerations which
detain him, when the stars are invoked on his account,
he replies that he is from *another* country, from the
heaven that has just been swallowed up.

The poet vivifies then hastens to the story's end.

At nightfall, despite his apprentice dimpled cheeks,
he is a courteous passerby who hurries his goodbyes
in order to be there when the bread comes out of the
oven.

ETERNITY

The life the death
of two things the one
or the grace of a goodbye

AWAITING
RETURN

All the way
home from
Kyoto to

Boston
to see my
mother

dying to
sit in
a small park

in snow
in May by
myself

to toss on
leaving
a ten-yen

coin to
a budding
cherry.

Why should I
think of her
now? But then

she was my
mother. She
thought of me.

We have to die – to
learn that discipline
before we do our

selves under. You think
I'm joking – that the
words are only placed

in different ways
saying the same thing –
but it isnt that

simple. Or perhaps
I'm wrong and it is.
But death's not dying.

DREAMING LI PO

Death leaves no more tears
Life leaves more and more
This country sickness
No word – the exile –
Old friend – in my dream
Clearly always here
You are swept up there
How could you have gone
I fear you are lost
Beyond all distance
You came green wood time
You return all night
The moon falls fills home
Perhaps lights your face
Water deep waves wide
Don't let yourself drown

TU FU

FABULOUS

Just as I
say this the
light across

the way meant
to stay the
night goes out

and I must
find meaning
in darkness.

Flower
even
as you
do
  fade.

Forget alone and
forget you have forgotten –
have it both your ways.

14 OCTOBER 1970

I wept. Then felt my back sweating,
my clothing rumpled, my hand flatnosed.
I wanted some fur on my limbs,
so that your embrace be
like all true embracing:
the gift of a wild beast

JANOS PILINSZKY

'The Vista'

We stand on the mountain
turning towards ocean
and back into the earth,

feeling the sky more air
and the body frailer.
The hawk only each sees

descend in a long
circle into the pines
to brood among shadows.

THE
DIVER

The diver caught *au ralenti*
describes a spidery arabesque
and in that figure perhaps is one with
his life. One who stands on the springboard
already dead, dead the one who comes back
swimming to the ladder after the dive,
dead the one who photographs him, the unborn
who celebrates the event.
                                      And is the space
then alive in which any living thing lives?
Pity the eyes, the objective,
pity everything that gets manifested,
pity him who leaves and him who arrives,
pity him who makes out or has made out,
pity him who doesnt know nothing and all
are two veils for the Unutterable,
pity him who knows it, who says so,
who is ignorant of it and gropes in the darkness
of words!

EUGENIO MONTALE

Every morning
nothing more of the leaves heard –
the wind is voiceless –
as if the night had spoken
and the heart of man had stopped.

However the wind diminish us, re-
duces us to a thread, to learn in
our deserts, to learn to ride a
grain of sand.

I am banged up against the horizon.

Downtown morning rain sets dust
Outside the inn willows green
Drink much as you can with us
Once you're gone there's none to touch

ROUND
THE WORLD

Under the
pines the arched
bridge square pond

the keystone
stepped on found
teetering.

No scent to
the cherries
or the snow

and yet there's
a fragrance
that much more.

I will tell you the secret.
Listen.

What is it? – you ask?

I keep telling you:

Listen.

Merciless indeed
under the ancient helmet
a cricket crickets.

Ask me when
I am dead
the meaning

of this. Then
each word will
answer you.

POINTLESS
this dying
to be
what one is.

PIERRES VERTES / GREEN STONES

To fall asleep in life, to be woken by life, to know death, leaves us indigent, the mind/spirit corroded, the body battered.

Don't testify, don't reply that the day's contribution is much too feeble in us. You spoke like this already on the threshold of our old Lethe lodging house.

A spark destroyed my leather apron. What could I do? Leather and ash!

'Go away' – she says pointing at me – 'Don't take to heart my flowering apron.'

The imprecision of time too has to be lived. As the overgrowth of the word.

RENÉ CHAR

89

You quote my own words to me
and I think they must be yours –
they are beautiful. Of course

they are yours – as they return
through your affection. I wish
all our words could be so shared.

HOW
DO

I want the words
so simple and
true you feel they

have come out of
your own mouth and
are breathing you.

Sometimes one eludes....Is this the
reason why – from sunrise to sundown –
the day shows not a wrinkle?

To lend one's voice to one's own
silences does not do away with
curtailing.

FACTS
Current reading
For the use of great beginners

XXXII

One summer night, two men are playing chess on the bridge of a ship. Suddenly the full moon, emerging from amidst the clouds, projects so perfectly the shadow of the pieces at their feet that the players stop to follow this second game which has begun beyond their knowledge and in full scale.

Indeed, the pieces stand out not only on the bridge with confounding clarity: animated by the double movement of the rolling and pitching, they grow bigger, eat each other up, hurl themselves upon the players themselves then, beyond measure, become for an instant hesitant and fall back while becoming smaller. They then start to rotate, taper out, wobble, lie down, get tangled up, before surging once again from the shadow.

But the two men notice now an extra piece: a bishop, or a queen, changing place on the diagonal at a speed such as , as far as they can see, owes nothing more to the ship's movements: the shadow of a man upon the bridge.

MARCEL COHEN

93

XXXVIII

Neglecting to wear his safety belt, while he works often alone on the rooftops of Paris buildings, a roofer admits embarrassedly that his forgetfulness owes nothing to laziness: he is just trying to please his kids, accustomed by television to more amazing trades.

They take me for an aplinist, he explains, but, without the danger of falling and getting killed on the sidewalk, I am no longer anything in their eyes.

XLI

A man wonders what elementary solitude he is still looking to preserve (and with what strange feeling of shame) when he thinks himself obliged to explain that he has just spent an hour in carrying out unpleasant tasks, while in reality he observed, stretched out in the grass, as he did as a child, the charge of a legion of red ants against the cohorts, continuously renewed, of an army of black ants.

LV

Night after night, when he turns off his bed lamp before going to sleep, a man rediscovers this thought provides such a spark that he cannot succeed in suppressing it despite all the day's difficulties: as if a slow maturation, beyond all consciousness, really occurs during sleep then, and as little as it may be, it isn't quite the same man who is to awaken on the morrow, nor altogether in the same world.

LX

A man rising in his bed one morning violently tosses off sheet and cover, opens his ryes wide and settles back against the pillow even while still feeling crushed by the nightmare from which he has just been drawn. In his dream the sheet he has thrust aside, he drew on the contrary over his head while crying out. The image is of an absolute clarity since it's at the moment he cried he had awoken. However, he's not been able to decide if he really cried or if he thought he had cried out in the dream. What had he just seen? He is totally unable to say. Perhaps he was even dreaming that he had had a nightmare. Is it possible? In which case he would just be awakening twice and it's from a third space, more and more hypothetical and yet quite real, that he would be trying to draw himself.

The man, in any case, is awake enough to understand that, failing to exorcise the night, he cannot rise to day unscathed.

LXI

In the Tuileries, at the little pool where tiny sailboats
float about, a man remembers how, as an adolescent,
he was bent, for days, upon a piece of wood to give him
the form of a boat. His father had helped him in providing ballast. His mother had sewn the sails. Nothing
had ever seemed more beautiful to him than this sail
boat. Blinking he saw it, set on his night table, in the
dimness, which seemed to emerge so gloriously out of
some tempest.

Alas, hardly had he set it in water, even here, than
the boat had turned over, no doubt unbalanced by its
mast. The rest of the afternoon had passed watching it
shift about in the dirty water while noisy children ran
every which way to prevent their sound hired boat,
running straight into the wind, from coming up against
the curb.

It is less the memory of his humiliation that the
man now rediscovers than that of a pain whose nature,
for the first perhaps this very day, he had begun to become aware of: all the encouragements of his parents,
all their love as well, never came to more than a silly
viaticum against the most crying injustices.

MARCEL COHEN

LXVIII

Few things, he explained, had seemed to him more disconcerting than the collective intoxication of the Japanese, in April, before the blossoming cherry trees. One full moon night, he recalled, he had even seen two couples picnicking under the one cherry tree in a cemetery beyond a suburb simply not to miss the rain of petals falling upon them at the least rein-forcement of the breeze which, apparently, would have denuded the tree before dawn.

In Spain he had been gripped in the same way, at a late night hour, by the extraordinary power of a *saeta* which, without any doubt, was starting to awaken a good half of the town of Cuenca. During Bridge of the suicides, joining the two rocky spurs on which the high town has been built, he had caught a glimpse of the singer below, no doubt quite astonished himself, in the narrow half-darkened valley, by the resonance of his sarong at the foot of the cliffs. Only a Gipsy was capable of such impudence, making an unknown be noticed. Who would therefore dare to complain of being awakened by a prayer to the glory of the Virgin, even at so incongruous an hour?

MARCEL COHEN

LXXI

An adolescent writes a message telling of his loneliness, his feeling of suffocation, all his thirst for love
as well, adds his name and address, locks it into a bottle
and throws it into the sea.

Some weeks later, on a day of high high tide, on a
beach, he notices a bottle caught between some rocks.
He goes to it and recognizes his message. A bit embar-
rassed, as if he suddenly were found exposed naked to
the eyes of passersby, he gets ready to pick up his bottle.
But just then two young girls get there before him, start
looking for a corkscrew and then set themselves down
to read the message. The adolescent followed them
and, seated on the sand, hears them now laughing out
loud imagining the response they are preparing to send
to him.

One falls and all at
once a second has fallen –
camellias like that.

THE
BACON

Now as you die you

wonder what it was
all supposed to be

about – as if it

were not yet brought home
to you how dying

a life a life is.

No chance of
any
return

You the
absence I
have to face.

for Len

No way
out of it
yet

yet
out of it
we come.

LORINE

The water
did brim to
her back door

I see her
still in the
empty boat

moored there though
she herself's
ventured forth.

'froggy'

At any given

moment leaping into the

one eternal splash.

To be enchantingly alone. But does
that make any sense?

What we are, we are, most of the time,
thanks to what hasnt completely occured.

'Thanks to Zuckerkandl'

Here is the
word, *there* is
what it means

Each exists
by itself,
word without

thing and thing
without word –
you and I

without each
other: *here*
together.

From the hills a breeze
reaching a windbell thinking
of wanting to live.

TANEDA SANTŌKA

Once again to have
been being outdistanced by
an autumn evening.

WHO FOR US TOLD TIME,
he counts yet.
What has he to count, say?
He counts and counts.

No cooler will it get,
nor nightier,
nor wetter.

Just what helps us listen:
listens now
for its own sake.

———————

THIS EVENING TOO

Full,
there snow too upon this
sunswumthru sea has fallen,
ice blossoms in baskets,
which you to the city take.

Sand
you warrant swap for,
for the last
rose at home
wants this evening too to be fed
from trickledown time.

PAUL CELAN
———
III

THE SPRUNGFREE
grayparrots
celebrate Mass
in your mouth.

You hear it raining
and think, also this time
it's God.
_____

KNOCK the
lightwedges off:

the swimming word
the dawn has.

THE TORTOISE

Always to want to
go back, to correct
an error, ease a

guilt, see how a friend
is doing. And yet
one doesn't, except

in memory, in
dreams. The land remains
desolate. Always

the feeling is of
terrible slowness
overtaking haste.

I feel I must

apologize –
there's just no end

to me: I go

on and on like
this – if only

you – you – let me.

You are welcome
to my funeral –
some who cared

placed a rock
and flowers and
celebrate the name.

No poetry – please –
beyond that
of your shadows.

LA VIEILLE

All she can do
to get herself
and her chair

down those mossy
concave stone steps
in one piece

to sit by
the river where
boats moor where men

troll afternoons
and news drifts
the drugged waters

Herself she dreams
and the stream draws
nearer yet

Now that she's there
now that she's here
why not rest

why should she move
(she doesnt ask)
she doesnt.

Existing

is neither
a right nor

privilege

nor any
thing but a

miracle.

And now the
words – remote:
another

life, not this
obvious
makeshift. I...?

Dont tell me
who I am,
let me guess.

Like a child again
holding a round stone
in my hand until

the warmth of my hand
warms the stone and I
feel comprehended.

VEIL

There is no sun.
There is no moon.
And no childhood.
And above all no land, no mother-land.

There is no coffin and no homeland.
No cradle and no bed made,
death settled under our heads.

One who lives is on a pin point,
and our peace itself is nothing
but a busted worthless wing,
a bride's veil, off or not,
lost upon a nail.

Dangles.

We dangle.

No graveyard.

JÁNOS PILINSZKY

Stop killing the dead
and stop crying
and listen to them –
their undying

They hardly whisper –
make no more sound
than the grass does
growing where none pass.

GIUSEPPE UNGARETTI

HOW

Transcend time, or destroy it?
By destiny's will, or chance?
Together, or by one self?

So they ask themselves content
that no answer ever comes....

VLADIMIR HOLAN

Is there any one of us
human beings capable
of being truly human?

Understand me: I dont mean
humanitarian or
humanist. I mean human

as in human animal.
To die in the full knowledge
of death as ultimate – not

as ultimatum – to live
in the faith of living what
a mother and father gave.

What is life
a man asks

Only a
man replies.

THE
COUNTER

talking, the
two of us only,
over soup,

Mischa, it's
his place, raises
the question of

water, how
this guy comes in
for coffee in-

sists on a
glass of water, 3
glasses full

as if he hadnt
enough, alone,
to do

borrows a
toothpick and –
and asks for the key

to the john, that's
an awful lot
for a dime

'in this' he nods
'I know
I am right.' I say

nothing. It's good
to be wrong too
sometimes. But

never argue with
one who
has to be right.

In the nail box
all the nails
bent.

The world is not theirs:
they are animals.
You're sentimental.

I'm sentimental.
The world is not ours:
we are animals.

MY OCCUPATIONS

I can rarely see someone without beating him.
Others prefer a monologue interieur. I, no. I
prefer the beating.

There are people who seat themselves facing me
in a restaurant and say nothing, they stay for
some time, since they have decided to eat.

Here's one of them.

So I grab him, whack.

So I grab him again, whack.

I hang him on the coatrack.

I take him off.

I hang him again.

I take him off again.

I put him on the table. I squeeze him and choke
him.

I dirty him, I drench him.

He revives.

I rinse him, stretch him out (starting to get
excited, must be done with this), I massage him, I
press him. I compress him and stick him into my
glass, and openly toss the contents on the ground,
and tell the waiter: 'Now get me a cleaner glass.'

But I feel sick, I pay the bill promptly and
beat it.

HENRI MICHAUX

130

Anyone can play the poet –
get language to sit up and beg –
carry the news or lie down – all

feet at one's foot – making it seem
the easiest thing in the world –
as in a sense – if you can speak –

it is. But poetry occurs
in unanticipated ways –
bites and sniffs and keeps an eye on

spiritual territory.
Lets you know of what encroachments
bodies incur when they are free

of gross impediments. Enough
that when the poet himself has
done his thing and left his breath to

yours – you're not intended to sound
his praises – weep – or bestow on
him supervacuous honors.

THE LOCUS

Why say the idiot is not
a genius? He at least
knows nothing he does not
feel. The poorest fool
provides intelligence
a case of birth. And animal
is not the beast of scorn.
Consider the simple horse
ambling down the macadamized
Appian Way, under
the arch of flowering acacia,
not at all deterred
by notions of propriety,
slowing to drop dung
where other dung provided
precedent, as other time
other dung with earth.
Nor does the thoroughly-stained
sweatband of the contadino's
broad hat contradict
the brain concealed within.
Behind the small black eyes
more insistent than
mosquitoes in aimless aim,

amended by a gold halo
hung from the right lobe
signalling where angels may
fear to tread, no thought
has wormed its way except
through withered speech. OK.
One does not ask for more
when one sees always less.
We know too much and not
enough to touch place.
As the olive in ground so barbered
and rock-gutted, splits
upon its trunk, swallowing
pride, to spit up seed
in season, to purge the earth
of a little death. Oil
from the limbs for the limbs of life.
Genius? Nothing not
native to the soil –
indigenous even if indigent.
Each day a day's work,
an ideal the wisest man
has not yet formulated
into truth,
         as the earth has.

KARMAL
FUDGE or
: JUST
PLAIN
SLUDGE

1.

Avoid evil
even if crowned with wisdom.
Isnt a diamond-hooded cobra
most dangerous of all?

2.

Before doing anything
good or bad –
consider – wise one –
the likelihood.
The result of acts
hastily performed
a poison dart
piercing to the heart.

3.

You got it all –
but do you get it?

4.

Do your damnedest
you aint done nothin' yet.

5.

You're great –
no doubt of it –
but what good
does it do you?
What good does
it do us?

6.

Security
is the fear
of the rich.
And nothing
is secure
from fear.

7.

To tarnished eyes
all that glitters
or glimmers
is gold.

8.

The gods are
determined –
as obdurate
as hell and
as fulfilling.

9.

Sun and moon and earth
overshadow each
other and light is good.

10.

Poet – let
the words you have lived
give life to others

and you will have lived
beyond all other
poetry.

11.

For all the abundant air
you can only breathe one breath
at a time.
And you cant save it up.

12.

Fruit bends the bough
Clouds bring the rain –
Enough proves more
than enough is
enough for one.

13.

He tethers a tiger
with gossamer -
cuts diamonds
with a petal's edge –
sweetens the sea
with a lick of honey
who thinks to improve
man with word-money.

14.

Fools and sages
learn to put up
with each other
best silently.

15.

We are all poor
lavishing
ignorance
on each other –
the little wealth
preserving us
this common breath.

16.

Born is the mother
Only the mother
is born.

17.

Few words but those few loved
Spoken quietly – with care.

A crescent moon and
the earth turning hazier
buckwheat flowering.

Touring the world
tilling a small field
to its limits.

God the only way
we have of saying
nothing and all and

saying it with love.
Tree bird sky sea sun
gathering the word.

It doesnt
have to be
Jesus. Christ

is an
infant in
any old

arms in a
temple touched
by the light.

Sky earth sapphire and
rust. Only to look –
your royal highness –

for value at a
jewel – only to
read antiquity

from a book. The cost
festers and we cry
music – we cry word.

THE
LAMP

What else is
this? Reading
the darkness

of the word
by the light
of a page.

tall grass light wind bank
high mast lone night boat
star hang flat land vast
moon float big stream flow
name how bright art known
rank due old ill dropped
drift drift what which like
sky earth one sand gull

The tide
goes out
and

leaves the
island
land.

'The Mystery'

Swallows, how they
hightail it
skimming the tight
street,

swerving
just where the street
runs out. How each
pursues

each,
pursued
by a green sky
as the sun settles

desperate
to let themselves
go, O
against night.

'so easily'

Wind sweeping
the willow
and willow

the wind but
neither can
be brushed off.

SENGAI

149

'psalm xliii'

Come
to the hills
and in their

shadow and
light feel well
come.

with odor of plum
bursts the sunrise
mountain path

Follow
the stream:
Dont go
but be
going.

I picked a
leaf up

it weighed
my vision

I knelt and
placed it

almost
where it was

'... as he came so he went, and none did know whence he came or whither he went....'
—Villani

Every blossom
falls away to reveal there's
more to it than it –
but what that it is remains
for more and more to unfold.

Only a bunch of
swallows over and over
the darkening stream.

The dragonfly can
hardly stay the sway atop
that blade of a grass.

To embrace
a tree – how
silly can
one get – yet

To want to
dance with it
the way the
wind's doing.

Bell sound
bell silence

Who listens
listened

mountain
quietness
quieting
rain

TANEDA SANTŌKA

157

Just following the

mountain path – discovering

just this violet

In the hills
for a few days –
couldnt write

Gone further found
less – maybe
you know the place

FOR
JANG JOE

Like trying to
imagine a
butterfly

trying to
imagine being
a butterfly.

A snap
drop rain
leaf

To touch
attain
tinge.

MAEHWA

Spring at the twisted plum tree
Blossoms return exactly
But the late snow slows intent

———

Should I let go or still dream
Either way is difficult
Say – my dear – and I will know

———

HANU

Cold in bed with my green quilt?
No reason to freeze tonight
Sleet'll melt you there tonight

'Hanu' puns – her name – on the word for 'sleet'

no name for the tree

whose blossom this is

fragrance only

The leaf that moved with the wind
moves
with the stream.

THE RITE

To say sky
as one says
water. To

pour it in-
to a cup
and hold it

at the lips
and drink. Of
it. And at

sundown to
drink it a-
gain as wine.

Almost

almost –

reaching

across

the night

the stars

CRICKET

On that occasion
with only sagebrush under
serving as pillow
the scratchings of just this bug
close to being sweet to me

SAIGYŌ

167

Sun in
the window –
an eye

for an
eye awa-
kening.

morning-dewed
streaked cool
muddy melon

BASHŌ

opening the window
a window full
of spring

Of course,
life matters.
Twitter,

sparrow,
and let me
know it

The beauty
of a rose –
one petal

enfolding
another
unfolding.

Is it the leaf
cradling the
air or air leaf?

How gentle
this falling is
together.

A
cricket

making
it

The
cricket.

Two pairs of black dragonflies
escort me as far as the gate
these mornings, as if I didnt
know where it was they are I'd be

ALREADY

Touched by weeds

passing along

a narrow

sidewalk.

The splendor
of a dew

About all
there is to

this.

FOR

a
moment
a leaf

higher
than the
tree.

Pointing out
each rain drop
in the field
the sun light

remembers
all is just
the smallest
part of all.

PHILANTHROPIST

Pissing in
the river
in the rain.

In the flood's
confusion
the shadow
of a bridge.

Leaf by leaf
returns to earth –
no one counts –
the number is
too well known.

I eat my morning rice.
I see the morning glories.

Morning glories
enough thatch
for this hut.

The goldfish
rest touching
each other.

AREAS OF INTEREST

the telephone keeps ringing
the clouds hardly move

There are things to be said. No doubt.
And in one way or another
they will be said. But to whom tell

the silences? With whom share them
now? For a moment the sky is
empty and then there was a bird.

You are

the rock

shadow.

To sit in the room
without a light and
feel the evening come

over the garden
into the house. To
feel it coming home.

Without a bowl
both hands
receiving.

OZAKI HŌSAI

Alone but
the mosquitoes
won't let me be.

KYOTO
GARDEN

What would a cricket

be doing at the end of

the year here? What do

you think? It is there and there

is where it's celebrating.

A red
thread

on
and at

the no
stage.

The year's first snow
building upon the building
up on the bridge.

The snow light brightness
and the house completely
quietness.

TANEDA SANTŌKA

194

On the swept pond
snow sets
out

No longer
hearing
snow

fall
now that
night's fallen.

FUJI

Between

heaven
and
earth

one
snow
mountain.

Quiet day – nothing

seems to be happening and

all is accomplished.

The sky is
the sky

for a
long time now.

THE MAN WHO ALWAYS WAS

breath never left off

I'm of two minds about selecting Cid Corman's poems, and no wonder given the man!

On the one hand we all know his output was tremendous, but I don't necessarily believe that means we have to measure our own scale by his dimension. Cid could be redundant in his explorations, and I find no fault there; it merely meant he was ever cutting away, searching, drawing, sketching. Think of a skilled woodcutter shaping a forest. It brings up for a great deal of wonderful reading.

At the same time, he was a sharp editor, razor sharp, and would produce his own journal *Origin* at an even 64 pages each issue. The majority of his books were back-pack marvels – packed light for the long distance traveler and the narrow trail. Scaled down. Plus his domain and mind was Kyoto and his practice amongst the natives was humility, silence, space, *less is more.* He wasn't always wise with it and would blabbermouth into whole scale marketing of thousands of poems, but he meant to be wise. And quiet. I'd like to think we are not making as much a representative selection here, but a philosophical one practicing the less is more and at the same time presenting the highest quality of Cid's poetry summing up that force of goodness. It's definitely an edgy approach. What's 500 poem pages of expanse, compared to the experience of reading Cid Corman in one warm flush sitting. As a poet, he would forever advocate how one poem can be enough, providing space around that one poem, so *resonance be allowed*. We, as editors, are simply allowing Cid Corman to practice what he preached.

Cid Corman lived the last forty years of his life, last days, last very seconds in Kyoto, Japan with his Japanese wife, Shizumi. They resided in a tiny and marginal location that others who visited knew much better than I – having never visited, myself, except by letter, and quite often Cid and I exchanged letters two to three per week for years on end. This was long before email correspondence which Cid only learned to use sparingly. He was already a massive correspondent and daily writer of poems, and one day more of the world will know this through his vast unpublished and printed works. The books range up to two hundred titles (peanuts for a man who claimed to write a book a day), and the unpublished works are scattered amongst fine libraries and institutions. Get in on the secret: Cid Corman was a major poet, translator and editor of the twentieth century. He was well over six feet tall, generally out of shape physically but immense with energy, strength, and character. His bald head was often capped over with a beret which looked quite bohemian on him, and this was correct since Cid spent some of his early years in France and Italy living out of a suitcase, slumming with poets and artists and sometimes souls of poetry who wrote nothing, but *lived the poem*. These were Cid Corman's people.

Cid Corman was raised in Dorchester, Massachusetts in

a now dangerous neighborhood he would barely recognize. All his life he adored his parents, Abraham and Celia, and his two brothers Harvey and Len; strangely, his sister Sylvia is less spoken of in his poems and autobiographical prose. Nonetheless, they all played a major feature in his development as a poet. They each kept him alive, often financially, and particularly with his two brothers there was a shared existence. His one wife for life, Shizumi Konishi, would inherit the same love Cid gave to his mother and father and siblings and closest friends, and despite the often shabby treatment of Cid by some of his colleagues – if Shizumi was by his side, all was well.

Cid could be difficult, or at least singular, like all fascinating critters. Complex and simple. Grainy and smooth sailing. One moment ornery and glacial, the next moment pacific and nectar, it all depended on his axis. He seemed to think in the old Japanese tradition of the apprentice and the master – Cid of course being the master to many of the younger poets that arrived in his mailbox or at his door after the loudest wave of Asian influence came crashing the shores in the 1960s via the works of Gary Snyder, Kenneth Rexroth, Alan Watts, and of course the Vietnam War. There was something gem-like and sparkling to a Cid Corman poem, learned himself from the myriad of poems he translated from enriched world poets. He never stopped finding known (but made new) and unknown poets to bring to English.

Things to know about Cid Corman are that he never conceived any children, but he wrote wondrous poems completely fathered onto others' children, so made *his*.

The woodcutter and his son with waiting wagon in this book is one of Cid's quick sketch beauties taken from one of my letters to him and shared from my family work scene. He was quite capable of receiving love and returning it just the same. He much enjoyed *his* Boston Red Sox throughout his life, Japanese baseball, and sumo wrestling. He never learned to drive a car. He hitch-hiked, he walked, he waited. Almost every part of our letters had something to do with the Boston Celtics, world cinema (he enjoyed Bresson, much respected Meryl Streep and Shizumi has a thing for Jennifer Jones), and so many differing steppes of books to love. We papered our letters and conversation walls with books; one or two or three always in hand, we may as well have worn books as deep fluffy boots and shoes. One time we stood together in Scribners Bookshop in downtown Manhattan during an impossible dream visit that was true (he from Kyoto, I from Vermont) and just flocked for a hen house flurry hours flapping our wings over tons of books. What luxury. Two guys in from desert islands. He cared nothing about the books he already knew in that part of the conversation – he wished to know more and more about the new and younger poets he hadn't read. He was the opposite of grandpa: everything fascinated Cid, if but for a few seconds. The ingredients may all reappear in a letter from him in a year, so best keep on your toes.

For a man who never wore a tool apron, broke a woods trail, connected down down into a soft stump with an axe or snarled with a chain saw, Cid managed to attract himself to some of the wilder portions of a poetry life.

He translated old trail guide Bashō one of the best. He published Gary Snyder's first book of poems *Riprap*. He was friends for over a half century with the woodland & coastal Theodore Enslin. Louis Zukofsky was his own frontier, and Cid literally preached his poems to audiences traveling across America in 1960, about the same time Jack Kerouac was giving up on the road. Lew Welch, Philip Whalen and Will Petersen were friends; so was Robert Creeley (despite more sensational rumors) who once raised pigeons in backwater New Hampshire. Cid wanted my book *On Stone* about stone building and woods life and made it an Origin title, then he asked for two more books until it was a trilogy. And perhaps the wildest part about Cid – the pioneer of the man, the wagon master and pathfinder – was his work as editor with *Origin* from roughly 1950 to his dying moment 31 Dec 2003. Same dying day (but different year) as his discovery and friend Lorine Niedecker. And though it is true Cid hung on in a coma for three more months...he was *elsewhere*. He walked into the hospital a very sick man, and never walked out. The very last place on earth he ever wanted to die, that's why he was *elsewhere*.

When Cid wrote letters to me it was sometimes the only letter of the day in my rural mailbox, and there might be two in the bargain from him. Cid told me it was often the same case for him on his end: just my letters in the mailbox that day. What's this – two lonely guys? Or two guys fully involved. "About *what?!*" you might ask. I can just see Cid's beaming face coming through loud and clear and answering with the drama of a whisper: "it's about *poetry*." Like Orson Welles' "Rose-bud." It was all about poetry. *Breath never left off.*

When Ce Rosenow kindly asked me to join her in preparing a selection of Cid's poetry I offered two ideas: let's make this collection for the poets who don't yet know they're poets (check yourself out, you may be unaware), and that I might work best traveling along as her passenger. The sidekick who asks, "Did we miss our turn off?" or, "What a beautiful day for a drive!" And, of course, a passenger may just want another passenger and that's just where you, dear reader, fit in.

Cid was but one man, one neighbor, one friend. The last thing he cared about was recognition – it was either the Nobel Prize / or nuthin'. So truly: read these poems as yours. Share them with someone else to make them theirs. See if you can be nearly as generous.

— Bob Arnold

size of it–
pocket sized–
nothing the
breath won't fit

CID CORMAN